FIRST RESPONDER FINANCE$

GUIDELINES FOR FINANCIAL SUCCESS IN YOUR FIREFIGHTING, EMT OR LAW ENFORCEMENT CAREER

ROBERT LEONHARD, EA

www.vsfinsvs.com

Dedication

First, I dedicate this book to my dad, the most honest and best man I ever knew and the standard by which I measure all men and myself and find that most fall short.

Secondly, I dedicate this to all of the men and women who go out on the street and do an often dangerous and always stressful job.

Be Safe Out There!

Table of Contents

www.vsfinsvs.com

5

Why Did I Write This Book?

I wrote this book for YOU—yes you, the person who goes out there to serve the "public" whether they want you to or not. You put on a uniform that may include turnout gear, riot gear, a handgun, a stethoscope, or you may dispatch those people who do go out on the street—it doesn't matter for the purposes of this book. What does matter is that you have chosen a profession in public safety that a colleague of ours calls "the hardest jobs in America". Now we will certainly get arguments from many other vocations and professionals about that statement but regardless, the jobs are tough enough.

In my career as a firefighter, I have been an Advanced Cardiac Life Support instructor and a Pediatric Education for the Pre-hospital Provider instructor and I enjoyed both. I believe that if you have knowledge, information or training that can help other people, you should try to share that knowledge, information or training. I have been investing for twenty-eight years and I have been studying financial planning for most of that time. I want to share that experience and knowledge with my fellow public safety professionals in this short book. I truly love and am fascinated by this subject matter and I want to help you to understand the basics you need to be successful in your financial lives.

www.vsfinsvs.com

So, here is my key question to you:

You are willing to care for and protect total strangers and to put your life on the line for total strangers—why would you not be willing to provide the same care and protection for you and your family? Why indeed?

We all say we got into this kind of work to help people and that is a noble motivation to be sure, but at the end of the day, we all have the same goal: go home healthy and secure. I have written this book to get you thinking about your financial life outside the firehouse, patrol car, ambulance, emergency department, or dispatch center in those same terms: health and security. Let's begin.

I lean to the EMS side to provide an analogy of my financial and tax planning thesis:

1) Diagnose first. Determine your financial vital signs before prescribing a treatment.
2) Determine the most effective treatment.
3) Treat (act).

Of course, it's not really that simple but these steps are valid and essential and must be accomplished in the order above. For you shooters and hunters out there: would the following sequence produce your desired result? Ready, fire, and aim! It's the same with your tax and financial planning.

www.vsfinsvs.com

What This Book Is, And Is Not

I hope it is easy to read. I have done my best to keep it jargon free and clear. I found this quote by Chief Justice John Marshall of the US Supreme Court on clear writing, "The man who by seeking embellishments hazards confusion, is greatly mistaken in what constitutes good writing. The meaning ought never to be mistaken. **Indeed, the reader should never be obliged to search for it.**" My goal is good, clear writing and I ardently hope I have achieved that goal.

The financial world has its own "language" just we do in the safety services, and so I have used these terms where necessary. I have tried to keep each chapter to just a few pages. You can choose to read it cover to cover or just the chapters that apply to you at the current stage of your career.

I have used a broad brush to cover each topic. I wanted to include the critical elements that you need to consider as you progress through your career. There are no "step by step" instructions, complex diagrams, complex math (glad to hear that, aren't you?) or forms to fill out. In some chapters, I will refer you to other sources for more detailed information if you want to research the topic further. Much of the content applies to most anyone seeking to get better control of their finances and taxes, but some is unique to public sector employees and I will stress that unique content for you.

8

I have included an appendix of sources for further study and information all of which I have read and found to be solid and helpful to me.

Most of all, this book is a call to action for you. We are action-oriented people in the public safety services and I have tried to give you a general protocol that lays out the critical elements of your financial life that you should follow up on in greater detail on your own or with a professional adviser. I submit to you that a modest investment of time and/or money in planning now will reap rewards far in excess of the initial investment.

Caveat: this book is not a substitute for dedicated, thorough planning based on your research and learning or your time with a professional adviser. As I said above, there is not a lot of "how-to" in this book—that would require a book MUCH longer than this one! **Primarily, these chapters are the "should and must dos" for your financial life**.

The information is not made up by me; it is based on my reading, research, and formal study in the past twenty-eight years. The strategies and tactics included are not new for the most part, but are based on commonly accepted practices by practicing professionals and academic researchers in many fields of financial study and planning.

We public safety professionals accept ACLS guidelines, fire fighting tactics and policing tactics that we know have been developed and tested by fellow professionals in our fields— the information in this book is a composite of and derived

www.vsfinsvs.com

from the work and research of professionals from a variety of financial, economic and even psychological disciplines.

I am not reinventing the wheel for you— just trying to get you to take the wheel.

Why Should You Pay Any Attention to Me?

OK, you probably are wondering: who the heck is this character who is writing this? Glad you asked!

First of all, I am one of you. I have been a full time firefighter/paramedic since 1997. I am currently a lieutenant and EMS coordinator for my fire department. Now, my journey to this point in my life includes a few bends in the road.

I earned a Bachelor's of Arts degree in History and Archaeology in 1987 from The Ohio State University while working full time and earned a Master of Public Administration degree in 1992 from The Ohio State University. I wrote my graduate thesis on forming joint fire districts in Ohio and as a result of that academic study, I began consulting with local governments to help them investigate forming joint fire districts. My consulting work led me to my, current active role as fire fighter and paramedic.

I became fascinated with the financial world early in 1987 purely by accident after being solicited by a financial marketing company. I did not buy into the company's strategy (it was a multi-level marketing company like Amway or Avon) but I realized that I needed to learn about finances and investing and so I went to the library and started reading, beginning with Charles Schwab's <u>Be Your Own</u>

<u>Stockbroker</u>. I began investing in 1987 just in time for the largest single day drop in the history of the Dow Jones Average, to that point in history, in October, 1987. Even so, I realized that this was a wonderful buying opportunity and that I had the greatest investing asset on my side: I was only 30 years old and I had TIME. I also learned that I had discovered another intellectual passion besides reading history.

I completed the comprehensive financial planning course work from the College for Financial Planning in Denver, CO in July, 2007 and in March, 2009 I passed the 10 hour exam given by the Certified Financial Planner© Board of Standards, Inc. This was my second attempt at this exam, which was by far the most difficult I have ever taken in any area of my academic career. I took and passed the Series 65 exam offered by the National American Securities Administration Association, which permits me to perform in the state of Ohio as a registered representative of my own firm, Vital Signs Financial Services LLC.

In 2013, I completed the course work and passed all the examinations to become licensed by the Internal Revenue Service as an Enrolled Agent. **Enrolled Agents are America's Tax Experts;** EAs are enrolled to practice before the IRS in all matters. I am currently completing the process to become a Fellow of the National Tax Professional Institute, in order to be comprehensively prepared to represent taxpayers before the IRS in the most effective and thorough manner. To learn more about enrolled agents, please go the website: www.naea.org.

In my spare time I like to read about history, investing, financial planning and science. My wife and I love to travel and have visited many states in the United States and we love to go to warm places with beaches when it is cold. I also like to do woodworking. My future goals include learning to speak Spanish (currently under way), obtaining my sport pilot's license and to write more books.

Pre-plan Or Free-lance?

A man who does not think and plan long ahead will find trouble right at his door. ~ Confucius

Plans are nothing; planning is everything.
~ Dwight D. Eisenhower

Firefighters have pre-plans so they are prepared for the structure they are entering. EMTs have protocols we must follow in order to deliver the proper care based on our medical director's best practices. Police officers have very detailed procedures they must follow in order to protect the rights of their subjects and also that will allow them to provide the best information to the prosecuting attorneys for use in the court room.

None of these professionals just go by "the seat of their pants". That is not to say they do not rely on experience and learned knowledge—they do but they use this experience and knowledge within a set of best practices. "Free lancers", those who go their own way and don't work as part of a team or within a set of best practices make for exciting and compelling characters in action movies and TV shows, but they put themselves and their team at risk.

What does this have to do with your finances and taxes you ask? There are a set of best practices in your financial life that almost anyone reading this book should be following that allow you to pre-plan your financial decisions to reach the goals that you have set for yourself and your "team."

14

Who is your "team?" Your team is your family who depends on you.

In one of my absolute favorite movies, "A Few Good Men," Jack Nicholson's character says to Tom Cruise's character that "You have the luxury of not knowing what I know." Well, that also applies to what we do. The public only knows what they read and hear in the news and what they see in movies and on TV. They never have to see the abused children, the people who can't breathe but won't stop smoking, the drug addicts and all the other sights and smells we call a job (or job security). They have the luxury of not knowing, **but you do not and cannot have that same luxury in not addressing your financial life!**

If you choose to free-lance in your financial life, you can make quick, impetuous decisions now based on inadequate information, which seem not too serious, but can and probably will have serious, negative consequences in your future. We will discuss these best practices as we move through this book so read on.

So, be a pre-planner and protect yourself and your team!

Let's Start With Your Taxes

It's income tax time again, Americans: time to gather up
those receipts, get out those tax forms, sharpen up that
pencil, and stab yourself in the aorta.

~ Dave Barry

You may be leery of beginning with financial planning for a
variety of reasons: you may think you can't afford it; you
may think you don't need it, or maybe you think financial
planning is only for "rich" people—whatever. So, let's start
with your taxes, since we all have to pay taxes and no one
likes it or likes preparing them (well, people like me like
preparing them of course).

Regardless of whether you prepare your own taxes or you
take them to a paid preparer, each year April 15 represents a
review of your financial life for the past year, or it should
represent this. You have to do your taxes so why not use this
time as a review of your financial goals and your progress
toward achieving them?

Preparing your taxes accurately, thoroughly and legally so
you pay the absolute least amount of taxes you must legally
pay is the first and primary objective. I want to take a short
detour and talk about the range of paid preparers out there.

The strip mall preparers: you recognize these companies:
H&R Block, Liberty and Jackson Hewitt and others. I don't
claim to be intimately familiar with the requirements of these

companies except to say that they have their own education courses to train many of their preparers. Many people use their services and are satisfied with them, but I do not know whether or if they offer much in the way of year round tax planning.

Certified Public Accountants (CPAs): CPAs have a college degree or degrees in accounting and have passed a very rigorous exam to obtain the CPA license. CPAs perform accounting and auditing and many prepare taxes. They also can represent taxpayers in front of the IRS. Some CPAs do offer tax and/or financial planning services.

Enrolled Agents (EAs): many people are not familiar with EAs, but we are working very hard to change that. I am most familiar with this certification because I am an EA. EAs must pass an education course specified by the IRS and pass three examinations covering personal income taxes, business income taxes and representation before the IRS. I include a quote from a brochure, which is provided by the National Association of Enrolled Agents (NAEA) that describes what and who enrolled agents are:

What is an enrolled agent?
Enrolled agents (EAs) are America's tax experts. EAs are the only federally-licensed tax practitioners who specialize in taxation and also have unlimited rights to represent taxpayers before the Internal Revenue Service.

Enrolled Agents vs. Other Tax Preparers?
An enrolled agent is a person who has earned the privilege of representing taxpayers before the Internal Revenue Service

www.vsfinsvs.com

by either passing a stringent and comprehensive examination covering individual and business tax returns and representation of clients before the IRS or through experience as a former IRS employee.

Enrolled agent status is the highest credential the IRS awards.

Individuals who obtain this elite status must adhere to ethical standards and enrolled agents, like attorneys and certified public accountants (CPAs), have unlimited practice rights. This means they are unrestricted as to which taxpayers they can represent, what types of tax matters they can handle, and which IRS offices they can represent clients before. But unlike attorneys and CPAs, who may or may not choose to specialize in taxes, all enrolled agents specialize in taxation. CPAs and attorneys are licensed by the states, but enrolled agents are federally licensed. That means they are not limited to practicing in states from which they have received a license; they can practice anywhere in the United States.

Are enrolled agents required to take continuing professional education?

In addition to the stringent testing and application process, the IRS requires enrolled agents to complete 72 hours of continuing education every three years to maintain their licenses. The National Association of Enrolled Agents (NAEA) raises the bar even further – its members are required to complete at least 90 hours in a three-year period.

That ends the commercial for EAs. Thanks for tuning in!

18

Do I Really Need to Talk to a Professional?

The wise man is one who knows what he does not know.

~ Lao Tzu, Tao Te Ching

If you have ever been to the dentist, you recognize the tool above—just think about the sound it makes and you may get cold chills as I do. If you had one, you could drill on teeth but I doubt anyone would let you without being trained as a dentist! So just because you can buy the tool doesn't mean you're trained for the job. There are many other similar analogies: just because you can carry a gun and dress up in camouflage doesn't make you a soldier.

The point is this: it may seem expensive to invest a modest amount of money now to properly prepare for your financial goals and/or be sure your taxes are done thoroughly and properly, but if you make mistakes now, they will be magnified many times over in the future. Financial and/or tax planning can be very complicated and confusing and you

19

absolutely need to educate yourself on the complexities before you can use the many tools available or you can pay someone to help you.

You don't absolutely **have** to meet with a professional planner or tax preparer **if the following conditions are present:**

- You are comfortable dealing with the complexities of the ever-changing financial landscape and new tax laws.
- You have the time and resources to properly prepare your taxes and financial planning.
- Should you ever need to respond to or appear before the IRS, you WILL want a professional to represent you be he/she a CPA, EA or Tax Attorney.
- You know where and how to get the answers to your questions and problems.

I will pass on one story about myself. I know there is a huge amount of information online about travel arrangements, but I still work with travel agent, (Cindy Poling at travelwithme@yahoo.com) because I realize she has the expertise and time to get me the best travel arrangements and all I have to do is give her my plans. Easy!

As you read the following chapters, ask yourself: "Do I understand this material?" If you don't, ask yourself if you can learn it and apply it. If not, then seek a professional you feel comfortable working with. I suggest you consider a fee-only financial planner who only charges for the advice they

20

give. They are not selling any products for commissions and do not charge you a fee based on a percentage of your assets they manage for you.

I **strongly recommend** that you ask from whomever you seek advice: does he/she/they act as a **fiduciary**, which means he/she/they are **required** to have your interests foremost in all recommendations they make.

Your Financial Vital Signs

Your financial vital signs include the following items, which you can determine yourself or any qualified financial planner can assist you.

- Your total income, which you will know after you have completed your yearly income taxes.
- Your outgo: this is what you spend.
- Your assets: these are things you own, your savings accounts, investments, or anything else you own.
- Your debts: these are the accounts for which you pay regular payments to a creditor e.g. your car payment.
- Your Net Worth: very simply this is what you own minus what you owe. Net worth is the **real measure** of wealth not income. You can build a substantial net worth over time with your income from your public safety career.

Later in the book I share a formula that you can easily use to determine what your net worth should be based on your age and income. **I truly believe that if you plan properly, spend wisely, and save and invest diligently, there is NO reason you should not retire WEALTHY!**

What Do You Mean by Pre-Plans?

If you don't know where you're going, you'll end up
someplace.
~ Yogi Berra

Yogi was a wise man and a great baseball player. His point
is valid and critical: if you don't know where you're going,
any road will get you there and that "there" may be far from
what you envisioned when you were young. There are a few
critical areas that you must plan for.

Insurance

I know, everyone hates insurance except those who sell it.
However, insurance is one of those things you simply must
have to protect yourself sort of like turnout gear, bullet-proof
vests, and rubber gloves. Insurance is simply risk
management to insure you against catastrophic events. I said
there would be no complicated diagrams, but let me show
you a simple diagram to demonstrate basic risk management.

	High Probability	Low Probability
High Severity	Result is very expensive or harmful, so you want to insure for it.	Again, result can be very expensive or harmful; you want to insure for it or try to prevent it.
Low Severity	Cost or harm is low so you can retain the risk or avoid it.	Retain the risk.

The key is to be sure you are insured against those events that can have a catastrophic impact on your health, safety or property. At the minimum, you should have the following kinds of insurance:

✓ Vehicle Insurance. Please don't just get the minimum that is legally necessary but get the amounts that will make you whole if you have a serious accident and you need a new vehicle or extensive repairs.

✓ Home Insurance. You cannot get a mortgage without a good homeowner's policy so you will have to get this kind of insurance. If you rent, you can get renter's insurance for your property for a pretty low premium, so please protect your belongings from damage and theft.

✓ Health Insurance. If you are fortunate to have health insurance through your employment, great! If not, you can get insurance from the insurance exchanges via the Affordable Care Act. Regardless of what you think of this program, it does allow you to obtain insurance for catastrophic health events. Depending on your income level, you may be eligible for tax credits that will lower you premiums. The website is www.healthcare.gov.

✓ Life Insurance. The kinds and amounts of life insurance you may purchase should depend on your individual circumstances. If you have a job with benefits, you probably have a modest term life insurance policy included in your benefits. My opinion is that if you are single and don't need to leave a large amount of money to anyone, this is probably enough. If you died, and you have people you must provide for, then you are going to need a much larger death benefit. Please don't use "rules of thumb" to determine the amount of life insurance you need. Meet with a professional financial planner or an insurance agent you trust to do a detailed analysis of your insurance needs.

✓ Umbrella Liability Policy. While not truly essential, an umbrella liability policy supplements your liability coverage on your other insurance policies. You can

24

get a million dollars of coverage for a premium of around $150 per year. Your other policies must have certain, higher levels of coverage in place to get an umbrella policy, but these are the levels you should have anyway. We all hate paying insurance premiums, but please don't go "cheap" on your insurance. Get the best insurance you can afford from the best companies you can find. You could start your search for insurance company ratings with A.M. Best, which is a widely respected rating agency.

Emergency Savings Account

Before starting an investment program, you should accumulate a cash account that you can easily access with no penalties for withdrawing the money. There are many theories on how much you should have in this account. One commonly accepted rule is to have an amount equal to three months' expenses. Another rule is to have six month's expenses in the account. There is no hard and fast rule, but you need to accumulate this account. If you feel that your job is secure, you can have less money in this account since you are sure that you will have an assured income stream coming in for the future, and conversely, if your job seems less secure, you should try to accumulate a larger amount.

This money is for **emergencies!** A new gadget (phone, TV, etc), a new pickup truck or motorcycle, or a vacation are NOT emergencies! This money should be for the water heater that suddenly breaks down, or the water or gas line that breaks—bad things that you know could happen but are unexpected and not insured for. You can buy insurance for some of these events, but it can be expensive and these are events of low probability and moderate severity so saving for them is the best strategy.

You should save this money in a savings account or money market account (money market accounts are much like savings accounts in that the assets are denominated in dollar amounts). I recommend that you set up an **automatic withdrawal** from your paycheck into your emergency

www.vsfinsvs.com

account until you accumulate your desired amount. You can set these up so you can write checks from them, obtain a debit card, or transfer from them into your checking account. I know that you will not make much interest on them, but the point is to have the money readily available when you MOST need it. **Safety and accessibility** are the most important considerations.

Debt

A Lot of People go into debt just to keep up with those who
are.
~ Anonymous

To contract new debt is not the way to pay old ones.
~ George Washington

I hate debt and so should you. Let me qualify that to say I
hate bad debt. Debt is a tool and used properly, it can
enhance your life and allow you to enjoy your life. There are
any number of debt management and debt reduction books,
systems, plans and philosophies out there you can access and
follow and I have read about most of them. Perhaps the most
extreme system many of you may have heard of is the Dave
Ramsey system called "Financial Peace University." Mr.
Ramsey is a funny, entertaining (and in my opinion, a little
arrogant) speaker and writer whose system has helped a lot
of people get out of debt. He interjects a strong protestant,
religious tone to his advice that I find off-putting—money
and debt are agnostic. I have discussed his system with other
financial professionals and the consensus is that if you are in
dire straits with your debts, his system or one similar to it
may be what you need, but let's back up a little and discuss
debt and credit.

Obviously, if you want to buy a house, you will need to
borrow money for it unless you are independently wealthy (if
so, you probably don't need to be reading this book) or you
inherited a house. Mortgage debt can be classified as "good

28

debt" in that you are investing your borrowed funds into an asset that may appreciate in value but more importantly provides you with a home to live in and the mortgage interest you pay is a deductible expense for your income taxes. Mr. Ramsey would say that you should have NO debt beyond your mortgage, a belief that many respected financial planners disagree with (I also disagree with it). I believe that your financial capability and your personal discipline determine how much and what kind of debt you can incur.

Vehicle Debt: Most of us cannot pay cash for a new vehicle especially in our younger years. Ideally, your best course would be to find a good used vehicle that costs much less than a new one. There are several arguments for this: lower total cost; lower payments (or no payments if you have saved for it); lower insurance; and no immediate depreciation as with a new vehicle. I hate seeing newly hired firefighters immediately buy a new vehicle (usually a pickup truck) and saddle themselves with a substantial loan payment, or worse—a lease payment. **If you have to lease the vehicle, then you can't afford it.**

If you are further along in your career and can service the debt payments for a boat, RV, camper, etc. I believe you should indulge yourself since these vehicles can provide much enjoyment and relaxation from a high stress job. Just remember: they depreciate rapidly are not financial investments, but they can be investments in quality of life.

Credit Card Debt: This is the bad debt. I am not against credit cards. Credit cards make life easier and can be a source of immediate, emergency funds in many situations and/or locations. If you can pay off your credit card balance each month out of your regular income then you can responsibly use it while building your credit score. However, credit card interest rates are significantly higher than any other interest rates besides the "instant cash lenders" on the corner and if you allow your balance to grow and pay only the minimum monthly payment, it will take years to pay off the balance.

Use credit cards with discretion and care and they can be a good tool for your financial life and conversely, if abused, their use can create a financial hole that can hinder your goals and with excessive abuse can lead to bankruptcy.

I am not going to provide an exhaustive list of the various kinds of debt you can incur but I do want you to think carefully before incurring any kind of debt. The very best kind of financial planning you can do is to live within your means and toward that end I provide some standard ratios below that you can use to determine if you are managing your debt loads. These ratios come from the study material provided by the College for Financial Planning in Denver, CO to take and pass the CFP© exam.

- Consumer debt payments (vehicle payments, credit cards, etc.) should not exceed 20% of net **take-home pay**.
- Monthly mortgage payments (principal, interest, taxes and insurance) should not exceed 28% of gross income or one week's take-home pay. For example:

your gross income is $65,000 per year so your monthly payments should not exceed $18,200 or $1516 per month.

- Monthly payments on all debt should not exceed 36% of monthly gross income.

Controlling your debt is critical toward building a good credit score. A good credit score means you will get approved for loans and you will receive lower interest rates and even prospective employers may access your credit score. **A good credit score is precious—earn it and protect it!**

You should and can check your credit report for free at the website www.annualcreditreport.com. You can obtain a free report from one of the three credit agencies every twelve months so you could get a report every four months and never pay for a report (e.g. in January you get a report from agency A; in April you get it from agency B and then in August you get it from C and in January you start over again). You don't need to go to one of the companies who advertise on TV in those annoying ads.

Very Basic Budgeting

Nowadays people can be divided into three classes – the Haves, the Have-Nots, and the Have-Not-Paid-For-What-They-Haves.
~ Earl Wilson

Credit buying is much like being drunk. The buzz happens immediately, and it gives you a lift…The hangover comes the day after.
~ Dr. Joyce Brothers

Debt management, spending and saving all are part of budgeting: ugh, I know you hate the word like you hate taking calls in the middle of the night, but budgeting is a necessary part of meeting your financial goals. I do not believe in a meticulous system of recording every penny spent and allocating money for spending categories. This is tedious, boring and you probably won't start it and if you do, you probably won't continue it because it is tedious and boring. Here is a bare bones budgeting plan that has worked for me and my wife for over 30 years. Honestly, we have not had a serious argument over money since we have been married.

Before I lay out the budgeting plan, I suggest that you and your significant other, if you have one, try to determine if you are spenders or savers. If you are both savers, great! This should not be hard for you. If one of you is a spender and one of you is a saver, you need to have a discussion about priorities and I hope the spender is willing to move toward being a saver. If you are both spenders, you may need an outside person to help you work toward learning to save.

Here is the basic budgeting plan:

1) Determine what bills you must pay regularly. These are fixed expenses that can be monthly, quarterly, semi-annually, or annually, but they must be paid! Some examples are:
   - ✓ Mortgage or rent
   - ✓ Vehicle payment(s)
   - ✓ Utilities: (gas, electric, phone, cable, etc)
   - ✓ Insurance(s)
   - ✓ Other debt payments: credit card, student loan, etc

If you have one income, you simply have to plan to pay these expenses from that one income. If you have dual incomes, I suggest you divide the expenses as equitably as possible between the two of you (or three if you are simply roommates sharing living quarters). By equitably, say one of you makes $50,000 and one of you makes $25,000, then the higher earner would pay 2/3 of these fixed expenses.

The key point is to pay these expenses first! If you find that you cannot cover these expenses, you will need to look harder at how you are spending your income and you may have to make some tough choices about your priorities. **The most basic rule in financial planning is live within your means!**

33

2) Next: pay yourself! This is your savings and investments. I will discuss saving and investing in a little more detail later, but I cannot stress enough how critical it is to establish a habit of saving and investing. Conventional wisdom recommends saving 15% of your gross income. Even if you can't attain this level, start saving/investing some regular portion of your gross income.

Now, we are lucky that we are part of a pension system that will provide income in retirement and I will discuss how this fits into your saving/investing plans later in the book. Regardless, the pension will not provide 100% of the level of income you enjoy now so you will have to make up the difference if you want to have the same level of income in retirement that you have now. And there will be other goals you will want to save for such as an RV, a boat, college for your children, etc.

3) Now, the good part! Whatever is left over after paying your fixed expenses and paying yourself is for you to do whatever you want! This is the gravy. When you are younger, this may not be a large amount but it will grow as you make more income. My wife and I have always agreed that for this "gravy" what was mine was mine and what was hers was hers and it has worked. One caution: for large expenses, such as a new car, I strongly recommend discussing this purchase before committing to

it/them. I can guarantee that your wife will not appreciate you pulling up in the driveway on your new Harley that you bought without discussing it with her!

Tax Planning Or Overpay: Your Choice

I am thankful for the taxes I pay because it means that I'm employed.
~ Nancie J. Carmody

Dear IRS, I am writing to you to cancel my subscription. Please remove my name from your mailing list.
~ Charles M. Schulz (Snoopy)

Two very different sentiments for sure! My dad used to say that he wouldn't mind paying more income tax because it meant that he was making more money. Well, yes and no. It seems that the wealthiest among us pay the smallest portion of their income in income taxes. Why is that? There are many answers to that question and many will depend on your political and social beliefs, but one concrete answer is that those individuals almost certainly have done **tax planning**.

Taxes are certainty in our lives. Supreme Court Justice (and Union Army Officer) Oliver Wendell Holmes, Jr. said "Taxes are the price we pay for civilization," but it seems we ought to get a lot more civilization for the amount of taxes we pay! The point is that we have to pay taxes, but we should do our level best to pay the absolute least we are legally bound to pay and that requires some planning on your part.

Let's begin with your form W-4. When you are hired for any kind of employment you have to fill out a W-4 Form which will determine the percentage of your gross pay that you have withdrawn from your paycheck. It is important that you work through the worksheet included with the form to determine the most accurate withholding percentage. The worksheet will show you how many allowances to claim—the more allowances you claim, the less tax you will have withheld. Many people will take zero allowances in order to have the largest percentage of pay withheld resulting in a large refund—I do not recommend that you do this. It is always nice to get a large refund but you are giving Uncle Sam more of your pay than you are required and therefore giving him an interest-free loan of your money! Ideally, you want to owe nothing on your tax return but also do not want to receive a large refund; this means that you have paid what you owe but have kept what is yours.

Let's say you get a $3034 tax refund (the average refund for 2013 according to the IRS). This is money ($253 per month) you did not have during the year to spend, or better yet, invest. You could have made a car payment with this money, bought groceries, or put it to any number of better uses than giving it to the government! Let's say you invested $253 at the end of each month in an investment making just 2%: at the end of the year, you would have $3064—not a great return but you would have earned $30 rather than loaning that money to the government. We can play with a lot of numbers but just for S &G, let's say you invest that sum and get an 8% return in a stock mutual fund:

you would have $3150 and depending on where you invested it and depending on your adjusted gross income, you may owe no taxes on the return!

So, keeping the most of your income you can is the first tax planning tactic!

Some other tax planning tactics that all taxpayers can use are:

- If you own a house, deducting the interest and real estate taxes on your property.
- Contributing to a tax deferred savings/investment account such as our deferred compensation programs (called a 457 plan). This contribution lowers your taxable income.
- Taking advantage of deductions and credits for education expenses.
- Depending on your adjusted gross income, you may be able to deduct work uniforms, safety deposit box rent, union dues and other miscellaneous expenses that are deducted on Schedule A of your tax return.
- If you have very high medical expenses (I hope you don't) you may be able to deduct a portion of them, but this is one deduction you don't want.
- You can deduct qualified charitable donations such as donations to your church, the United Way, etc.
- If you invest, you may be able to deduct capital losses on the sale of capital investments.
- If you have a second job, you can deduct the miles driven from your primary job to the second job.

38

- If you have your own business, there is a much longer list of possible deductions. I will discuss this later in the book.

This is just a short list of possible deductions; you should consult with a qualified tax preparer or tax planner to discuss your circumstances. I advise contacting this person well before December 31 so you have plenty of time for thorough planning because on January 1 it is too late!

Investing

How many millionaires do you know who have become wealthy by investing in savings accounts? I rest my case.
~ Robert G. Allen

I will tell you how to become rich. Close the doors. Be fearful when others are greedy. Be greedy when others are fearful.
~ Warren Buffett

I confess I LOVE investing, specifically, in common stocks in stock markets in the United States and around the world. You may legitimately ask if I have made money in the stock market and the answer is a resounding YES.

I'd like to expand on the two quotes above: I confess I have never read any of Mr. Allen's books but the quote is valid. You cannot build wealth in savings accounts. There is no risk to your money in savings accounts, hence there is very little return. In the fire service we say we will risk a lot to save a lot. When investing, it is similar: you must assume some risk in order to realize gain.

Please don't confuse the movements in the stock market averages, called volatility, with risk. Most volatility is driven by the emotions of millions of participants in the markets, most of them classified as "professionals." Volatility is based on a statistical concept called standard deviation (you can Google SD for a further explanation or maybe you remember it from a previous statistics class) but it does not measure risk. Risk is the chance that your investments underperform and you do not reach your financial goals (I base this on a wonderful book called Behavior Portfolio Management by Professor C. Thomas Howard). Stock market volatility may look like a roller coaster but here I quote Dave Ramsey: "You only get hurt if you jump off the roller coaster."

For example: if you can get a 2% percent return in a savings account (which you cannot right now in 2015) and inflation is 2% per year (inflation has averaged about 3% historically), at the end of the year you have a zero real return on your money and you still may have to pay taxes on the interest, further eroding your return. You can see how over many years, the real value and purchasing power of your money goes down.

I think most people know who Warren Buffet is. If you don't, he is currently worth over 60 billion dollars, yes billion with a B! He made his money investing in the stock market (He recently bought a whole railroad! And not a "Monopoly" game railroad!) What he is saying is that when most people are afraid of the stock market, they sell and prices go down, and so this is the time to buy stocks when they are "on sale." When most people are greedy, stocks rise and become overpriced and so it may be time to sell to them or just hold on to them or you can wait for the stocks to go on sale again as they almost surely will. "Buy low and sell high" is the iron clad rule to follow but it is often hard to do. Many people panic when the stock market goes down, but this is a natural, historical condition and it means that stocks become more affordable.

One further example to illustrate this point: say you want to buy a house and the seller wants $150,000 for it but you think it is too high and you decide to wait. Something happens in the world that causes house prices to drop in your area and now the seller can only sell for $125,000. Do you say, "Well, no, I'll wait until the price starts rising before I buy the house." Of course you don't, that would be stupid! But many people will not buy stocks when they have dropped in price—what is the difference?

I include a story from my life to illustrate this point. I claim no unique talent or intelligence for my decisions, just a confidence in what I have learned in my life about investing and a confidence in our country and economy. In 2007, my wife was able to retire from her job of twenty-seven years where she had contributed to a 401(k) and she was fortunate enough to have a pension. We rolled all of her funds into an IRA in early 2008. You may recall that in the autumn of 2008 the stock market fell over 50%. I invested almost all of the funds in the IRA during one week when the Dow Jones Average dropped several hundred points. I had confidence that the government and the banking industry would do what was necessary to prevent a failure of our economy.

After reading the book and watching the movie Too Big To Fail, maybe I was a little too complacent, but we did dodge a huge bullet and the stock market subsequently bottomed in the spring of 2009 and entered one of the greatest bull

42

markets in history (the S&P 500 has risen from about 670 to around 2050 as I write, a 25% return per year!). This was my time to be greedy when others were fearful (and to be like Warren Buffet!) My main point is that if you sell when prices are down you turn paper losses into real losses and if you can buy when prices are down you can get some real bargains. Again, buy low and sell high.

Anyway, I am going to share my views about investing based on the dozens of books I have read; the hundreds of articles in magazines and journals I have read; the many speakers I have listened to; and my own twenty-eight years of investing experience. You can disagree with me but it's my book. I am not going to go into great detail about specific investments because there is a wealth of information you can access about these. Rather, I am going to present some general investing principles and guidelines that I have found to be valid either in my experience or by others' experience and/or research.

Just remember: investing comes after you have accumulated your emergency account and are covering all your fixed, regular expenses as discussed above.

I.   Decide what you are investing for; is it a down payment on a house; a vacation; your children's college; retirement, etc. The kind of goal and the timing of its achievement will affect how you invest and/or save for it.

II. Decide how much risk you can tolerate. The adage is "will your investments keep you up at night worrying?" A good investment adviser will try to accurately assess your risk tolerance. If he or she does not, then grab your wallet and run away as fast as you can go.

III. Be an investor, not a speculator. We cannot be concerned about what the market is going to do tomorrow. **We don't give a damn**. We are concerned about what your wealth will be when you need the money in the future for the specific goal for which it is intended.

IV. Don't confuse income with wealth. True wealth is represented by your net worth, which is simply the difference between what you own and what you owe. There are many people with high incomes that have low net worth because they spend most of what they earn (think about the stories you've heard about someone who owns a huge house in an upscale neighborhood with lawn furniture in their dining room).

    a. I know I promised no formulas, but this one is helpful and simple. In the book, <u>The Millionaire Next Door</u>, the authors provide a formula for determining what your net worth ought to be: **multiply your age times your realized pretax annual household income from all sources except inheritances. Divide by ten. This, less inherited wealth, is what your net worth should be.** Incidentally, I highly recommend this book.

44

V.   When you are young, you should invest in common stocks. Throughout history, common stocks have provided the highest return on your invested dollars. Since 1926 until 2001, common stocks have produced a 10.2% compounded annual return (from Stocks for the Long Run by Wharton Business School Professor Jeremy Siegel—another book I highly recommend), a compounded return higher than any other investment. If you had (or your parents or grandparents had) invested say $100 in 1926 and just left it to compound, it would be worth $515,204) in 2014!

VI.   Split your investment money between the Deferred Compensation Plan (the money is invested before it is taxed and taxes are paid when you withdraw it) and a Roth IRA (money invested in a Roth IRA is taxed before you invest it and you pay NO taxes when you withdraw it). If we knew what income taxes were going to be when you retire, I would say put all your investment money in one or the other, but we don't have this information so you can hedge your investments for the future.

   a.   Quick explanation: if we knew income taxes were going to be much higher in the future than today, we would just pay the tax now and put all the money in a Roth IRA and not pay any of the higher, future taxes. And if we knew income taxes were going to be much lower in the future than today, we would not pay the higher, current tax now and put all the money in Deferred Compensation and pay the lower, future taxes. **If only we knew**! And remember, you need to consider how much of your pension will be taxed in the future when deciding how to invest now.

VII. **Investing in the stock market is not like Las Vegas!** If you have confidence in our economy and believe that we will continue to create new products and services and new companies to produce those products and services, then you should be an owner of those companies through stock ownership. If you believe that the country is going to hell in a hand basket, then I have found Vance's Shooting Supplies to have the best prices on guns because that is what you will need to protect yourself, your family and your property. Even gold won't help you—you can't eat it or use it for bullets.

VIII. Finally, I suggest that you do not invest in individual company stocks unless you have the time and desire to research the companies. It can be a lot of fun to take a small part of your investing money and invest in individual stocks, but it requires work on your part.

IX. What about bonds? People have traditionally invested in bonds because bonds provide income and if you buy an individual bond and hold it until it matures, you get all your investment back. They are considered "safe" investments.

A quick definition: there are many kinds of bonds and the bond universe is **very** complex. Essentially what we think of as a bond is a

46

loan for a specific term that pays a specific rate of interest. For example, the bond issuer (a company, a government, or perhaps a hospital) sells you a bond for $1000, which is a very common amount for one bond, and promises to pay you 3% interest for five years. A typical bond will pay you this interest every six months so you will receive a check for $15 every six months (two payments of $15 each year for $30 total equals the 3%) for five years at which time the bond matures and you get your $1000 back and you have earned $150 in interest over the five years. Seems simple and a good deal right?

Here is the risk: bond prices fluctuate based on current interest rates. The full explanation of this fluctuation requires some moderately complex math and I promised none of that so here is the crux of the issue: when interest rates rise, bond prices go down and vice versa. Interest rates are very low (.25%) as I write this so if you were to buy bonds in a mutual fund or exchange traded fund as many of you would do, and interest rates were to rise which is the only way they can go at this point (2015), then your principal (your invested money in the bonds) would decrease. If you are not just nearing retirement, I suggest you keep your bond purchases very small until rates rise.

47

The 12 Universal Laws of Successful Investing

I was fortunate to meet a gentleman named John Stewart back in 2008 who had been a financial advisor for over thirty years and he invited me to work as an assistant in his office. Well, in late 2008 the financial and economic world damn near fell into another great depression and we did fall into the "great recession." I was privileged to view these events from inside a financial firm and it was not pretty but what a great experience.

John and I have moved on from that firm—me into my own fledgling firm and he to a firm called Physicians Wealth Solutions (www.physicians-ws.com); but we have stayed in touch and he has graciously allowed me to include the following laws in this book. These are laws he has developed based on his now thirty-eight years in the financial world. I have not included all the text but John assures me I have captured the essence of each "law."

1. The law of setting objectives: you must know your investment profile and set objectives tailored to your unique needs.
2. The law of risk vs. reward: you will have to assume some risk to obtain greater reward (see the quote about savings accounts above).
3. The law of diversification: diversification can reduce your degree of loss but it can also reduce

your chances of obtaining higher than market returns.

4. The law of concentration: this is the mirror image of diversification; sometimes over-diversification can lead to mediocre results and so conversely, you may achieve superior returns by "putting more eggs in one basket and watching the basket closely."

5. The law of establishing a stop-loss discipline: sometimes you just have to sell a losing investment. There may be many good reasons to do so, but too many investors try to hold on to the investment until they hope they can "break even," but sometimes it is better to sell and reinvest the proceeds into new, better investment.

6. The law of patience: you must be willing to stay invested and be patient. The markets tend to make significant moves over very short times but you cannot know when these times will be so you must be in the market to benefit from these movements.

7. The law of letting the winners run: simply stated, you keep your investments that are appreciating and let the gains accrue and if at some time, they start to go down you can choose a limit of loss (say 5-10%) at which you could sell and still reap the majority of the gain. Very rarely will you be able to sell at the extreme top or buy at the extreme bottom.

8. The law of compounding money: you will see a quote from Albert Einstein later about compound interest but suffice to say that your gains will grow based on previous gains and time is your greatest ally when investing as long as you regularly invest in assets that grow faster than inflation. Below is a graph of an exponential function, which is what compound interest is. I can't explain the math, but it shows how over time your money increases, well, exponentially! Amazing!

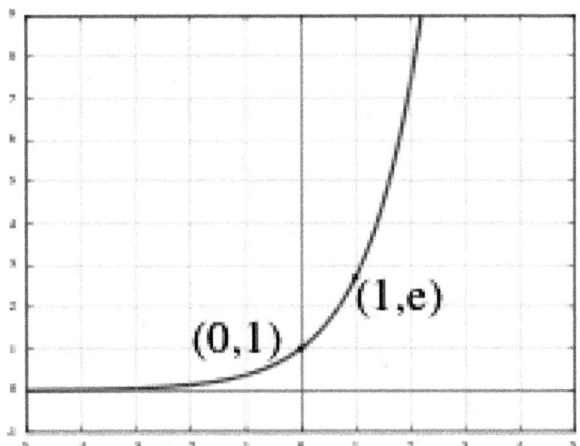

9. The law of prudent investing: You must have logical investing plan that will take advantage of compound interest. Benjamin Franklin said, "Money is of a prolific generating nature. Money can beget money and its offspring can beget more." Use your asset of time with compound interest to achieve success in you investing.

10. The law of purchasing power; the ravages of inflation: while inflation is very low as I write this book, it can and probably will increase in the future. You must invest in assets that can outpace inflation if you are to achieve a real return over time (see the quote above about savings accounts).

11. The law of frugality: start saving and investing early and develop the habits discussed earlier. Time and compounding are your friends— befriend them and take advantage of them and they will reward you.

12. The law of goal setting: develop your, unique goals and then develop a plan for achieving them. As Zig Ziglar notes in his book See You At the Top, you can't hit a target you don't have.

Please note: the laws are John's and the brief summaries are mine and I hope I did justice to them. If not, it is my mistake, because the laws are spot on.

Estate Planning: the Very Basics

The fear of death follows from the fear of life. A man who
lives fully is prepared to die at any time.
~ Mark Twain

Death and taxes and childbirth. There's never any
convenient time for any of them.
~ Margaret Mitchell: author of Gone With The Wind

No, death is not fun to think about or contemplate but in our line of work, death truly is a constant reality. We see those who have contributed to their own dying by smoking or engaging in other dangerous or harmful habits and we see those whose death came randomly and arbitrarily and much too often it came way too soon. We may have seen our colleagues die in the line of duty and this is always too soon and tragic. We of all people have no excuse not to be prepared for the ever present chance of our death. When you as a medical care provider answer a call on an elderly patient, what to you often ask: "Do you (or the patient) have a living will and/or DNR?" I ask a similar question: **"Do you have a will?" Do you have a living will? If not, why not?**

Everyone should have basic will and if you are married and/or have children, you simply must have a will—there are NO excuses not to have one! Your will instructs your executor (the person you appoint to carry out the instructions in your will) how to fulfill your wishes and instructions as to how you want your assets to be distributed to your heirs.

52

You also would leave instructions about who you would choose to raise your children if you and your spouse died. You can also include lots of other information about your assets and wishes, but these are the key ones. I recommend that you hire an attorney to prepare your will or at the very least you have an attorney review one that you may have prepared yourself.

These are the other, key, essential documents you should have in place. You can do some of them by yourself, but I suggest you pay the nominal attorney fee to make sure they are prepared correctly and thoroughly. If you do them yourself, at least have a lawyer review them. It will be money well spent.

- Name beneficiaries for your asset accounts such as IRAs, 401(k)s and brokerage accounts.
- Include bequests to specific persons for specific property you own; for example, you may have an antique desk that you want your nephew to inherent because you know he is going to be a lawyer. Record this so there are no arguments after you are gone.
- Get a durable power of attorney prepared, which appoints a trusted individual to handle your financial affairs if you are unable to do so.
- Get a health care power of attorney prepared, which appoints a trusted individual to make medical decisions on your behalf.
- Get a living will prepared, which explains your choices about end of life care.

53

- **You simply must have a will**, (I know I'm repeating myself here, but it is that important!) especially if you are married and most especially if you have children. The will directs who will get your assets and you can name the person(s) who would raise your children if something happened to both parents. If you die without a will, called *in testate*, the state may determine the above issues and **who in the hell wants the state to make these decisions for you?!**

GET A WILL PREPARED NOW IF YOU DON'T HAVE ONE!

Other Tasks:

You should have a list of all your key information prepared for your executor:

- ✓ List of all financial accounts with account numbers, usernames and passwords. There are a lot of free forms available for this and many good software programs also.
- ✓ You might want to write your own eulogy.
- ✓ Create a succession plan if you have your own business you want to pass on.
- ✓ Pre pay for your funeral so your loved ones do not have to worry about these decisions in a time of stress and grief.

- ✓ Visit the following website for wonderful help in planning your legacy: www.planyourlegacy.com.
- ✓ Prepare an inventory of your possessions. Again, there are lots of good paper and digital forms for this.

What About a Trust?

Some of you may have heard about trusts and may even have one or be a beneficiary of a trust. Trusts are beyond the scope of this short book and even I would not try to create a trust without the assistance of a good estate attorney. Trusts are a legal "container" into which you deposit and re-title assets. The trust becomes the owner of the assets and a trustee manages the assets on behalf of the beneficiaries.

There are many reasons for trusts and if you think you may need a trust, you absolutely should contact a good estate planning attorney or at least contact a financial adviser experienced in estate planning. The key to trusts is that you must fund the trust by re-titling your assets in the name of the trust and your designated trustee will manage these assets as your fiduciary which means that he/she/they must manage the assets with the beneficiaries' interests foremost.

I leave you with this thought: it is no fun to prepare for death, but as I said earlier, we in these professions in public safety are acutely aware of the fragility and randomness of life and death so I submit that the more prepared for death you can be, the less you can worry about it and enjoy your life, family, and career. So take the time to get these critical documents prepared (and remember to update them on a regular basis, especially as your life changes and gets more complex).

Now, with that out of the way, have fun, enjoy your life and career and let's move on to more pleasant topics.

Your Goals: the Basis of Your Planning

I was planning on my future as a homeless person. I had a really good spot picked out.
~ Larry David

I'm not saying that if you don't plan, you will end up homeless—I just think this is a really funny quote about planning. This will be a short chapter on setting financial goals that will determine how you invest and save. There is a whole industry out there on life planning, goal setting, etc. and I am not going to reinvent those wheels. I just suggest that you discuss with your significant other what your goals are and how you can achieve them. You may want to take a look at Zig Ziglar's book, <u>See You At The Top</u>, to be convinced of the need for good goals and how to set them. There's also a lot of just good advice in his book about life and a positive attitude such as, "Attitude, not aptitude, determines you ultimate altitude."

Short Term Generally these are things you want to get done within the next year. These are not goals that should require extensive research or financing. Some examples might be:

- Replacing carpet, furniture, or anything that you should not have to finance
- Taking a nice vacation
- Fixing anything that needs fixing around the house
- Starting to save for your emergency fund

- Purchasing all necessary insurance
- **Getting your will prepared!**

Medium Term   There is no hard and fast rule on what "medium term" means but I think these are goals that will require some research and may require that you finance them.   These may overlap with your short term goals especially when financing may be involved.   Some suggestions:

- Pay down any accumulated credit card debt
- Beginning your savings and investing program after paying down credit card debt
- Saving for a large purchase e.g. a house

Long Term   These are your dreams! Don't limit yourself here—have fun and dream big. There are a couple of long term goals that you simply need to prepare for, but they are still dreams. Suggestions:

- The biggest: Retirement. The earlier you start planning for retirement, the easier it is. I think retirement should be thought of as a transition, not a destination. Retirement is when you can do things without the constraints of your job.
- College for your children if you have them. I caution: **plan, save and invest for retirement first and then for college**. There are many sources for college funding but only you are the only source for your retirement.

- Starting a business. Many firefighters have second businesses on their days off and I know many police officers who become security consultants in various areas of specialization. A second business can have wonderful tax advantages.
- A vacation home or an RV
- A college degree for you or your spouse.
- Travel

Obviously, these lists are not exhaustive. You need to decide what your goals are, but those goals form the basis and framework for your saving and investing. Check out online, the library or a book store for goal setting systems—I know there are apps for that! There is a common system for setting goals called the SMART system and there is a lot of information and templates out there but here are the five keys to SMART goals:

- Specific: you have clearly spelled out what the goal is.
- Measurable: you know when you have accomplished the goal.
- Achievable: it is a realistic goal that you have the talent and resources to achieve.
- Relevant: it is important to you and/or your family.
- Time framed: you have set a completion date.

www.vsfinsvs.com

Where Are You In Your Career?

The worst days of those who enjoy what they do, are better
than the best days of those who don't.
~ E. James Rohn

I want to shift gears here a little bit. Depending on what
stage of your career you are currently in, your financial
goals, risks, and needs will be different. Just a few thoughts
before continuing because I have some gray hair and I think I
have gained some wisdom that may help you in your career.

First of all, I hope you can create a career, not just a job.
Anybody who has worked with me has heard me say that no-
one ever was drafted into the fire department and it goes for
other safety service professions as well. You CHOSE this
line of work so the organization that hires you expects you to
come to work ready to do your best.

There are many reasons to work in public safety services:

- Pretty good pay
- Pretty good hours
- Good benefits
- High regard from the public (most of the time)
- The opportunity to be on the front line of protecting
  people from fire, injury, crime, themselves, disease,
  etc
- Chance to work with a lot of other like-minded
  people

- You get to "play" with very expensive equipment and tools.
- You will get to see the world in a very different perspective from almost all other vocations with the obvious exception of military personnel.

These are all good reasons but to me the most critical reason is because you truly love the work with all the good and bad. You will get the opportunity to do things that most people only see in movies and on TV and most of them wouldn't or couldn't do it anyway, and you make it seem easy and routine; it may be routine, but usually isn't easy.

You will leave a lot of physical and emotional energy on the street (or in the hospital) and it can take a toll over the years so my charge to you is this: take the information in this little book to heart and work as hard to prepare for the day when you leave your career and begin a new chapter in your life as a retired police officer, firefighter, paramedic, dispatcher, nurse or doctor or whatever level of provider you achieved in your career.

You will have earned your retirement and it can and should be a safe and comfortable one if you prepare. So let's begin looking at a typical career path. I will use the fire service because that is what I am most familiar with but I am sure the suggested actions apply regardless of your chosen profession.

That First Job

Often your first job will be as part time employee or even as a volunteer. Let's assume you are very young and you have just gotten your first paying job. Things aren't real complicated at this stage; you are just trying to get your foot in the door, learn the job, get some experience and get your name known in a positive way.

Get Your W4 Forms Accurate

You are going to receive a paycheck or multiple paychecks if you have multiple part time jobs as many new, young members do. No matter what service you work in, it is important to get the W4 form filled out accurately. Often, with these early lower paid jobs, you can have too little income tax taken out at each job and end up owing a large amount in April.

The reason is that in each job you may only earn an income that places you in the lowest income tax bracket for that job, but when you add up all those jobs at the end of the year the total will lift you into a higher income tax bracket. Your final tax burden will reflect your total income for the year, not the several smaller incomes you actually earned from each particular employer. If you can't pay the whole amount owed in one payment, you can set up a payment plan with the IRS or you could put it on a credit card. Either way, you are in a hole that can take a long time to get out of.

Save <u>Something</u>

Start saving some part of your pay even if you only save $5 or $10 from each check; you will establish the saving habit. Don't touch this money unless it is a dire emergency! You will feel good at the end of the year when you have maybe a couple of hundred dollars saved.

Be Very Careful With Credit Cards

It can be very tempting to overspend on your credit card since you have income. Be careful: I don't believe you should not have a credit card at this point but do some research and find one with a very low rate, no annual fee and perhaps get one with a low maximum credit limit such as $500. Used wisely and discriminately, a credit card will help you build a good credit rating score. You can research credit cards at www.bankrate.com.

Buy A Used Vehicle

Please, please, please don't go out and buy a new vehicle just because you have some income. You can find a good, used vehicle and pay much less of your scarce income on it.

Remember, you are working these early jobs to gain experience, to learn how to do the work correctly and to build your positive reputation. I am not saying income is not important (I would never say that), but building your career is just as important.

Yes! You Got Your Full Time Gig!

What a sense of relief and exhilaration when you learn that all of the studying, testing and putting up with other full time employees at your part time jobs has finally has paid off! You still have some sort of probation period to work through (surely, you can behave for this period can't you? Sorry for calling you Shirley. Hope you got the reference to the movie "Airplane") but now you have attained a great deal of career security:

- Full time paycheck
- Health insurance
- Vacation (after one year)
- Sick time
- Overtime!
- Holiday pay
- Longevity pay (maybe)
- Compensation time (maybe)
- Training time paid for
- Union membership (maybe)
- Pension membership

Obviously, there are a lot of perks that go along with this new, full time job and a great opportunity to get started on a sound financial footing. I suggest the following, general plan for this new bonanza:

- DO NOT go out and buy a brand new pickup truck! Assume you want to buy a $30,000 pickup and you can get an interest rate of 3.5%. With no down payment (which you probably don't have since you have been working part time jobs) and a four year loan, your payment will be $671 or $8052 per year! Now let's say you can find a good used vehicle for $15,000; the same terms result in a payment of $335 per month or $4020 per year. If you invest the difference ($4032) and can get a return of 6% (which you can) at the end of one year you would have $4274. PLEASE don't incur a large debt in celebration of your new career!

- Instead of incurring debt, ratchet up your savings. Get aggressive and build your emergency account. Aim for a nice round number such as $5000. If you invest our hypothetical amount from above ($4032) every two weeks as you get paid ($155 per paycheck), it will take only about sixteen months to accumulate your $5000. Now you will have a nice emergency fund and lower debt! Feels good doesn't it?

- Now you are in your second year and no longer on probation so you can really speak your mind now! Seriously, now is the time to start working on your financial goals, which will affect how you spend, save and invest. I will cover some critical life events and goals later in the book, but for now I just want to emphasize the importance again of learning to invest in the financial markets. If you grew up in or experienced the years from 2000 to 2012 it was a wild ride. You may think the financial markets are rigged or just for the rich—neither of which is true. I explained my views on investing earlier in the Investing chapter, so I won't belabor the point here just to say it is now time to start investing for your goals.

Well, those are the key actions for your initial years in your new, full time position so lets' move on in your career.

Wow, I have five years in and I'm bearing down on the big 30.

Now you are into your career and I will bet that certain goals and events are foremost in your mind. Let's discuss some that most all of you at least have or are thinking about.

<u>Marriage</u>   I won't say too much about marriage except that I have been married for over thirty years and our marriage is the best right now it's ever been. It hasn't always been easy but the tough times have made the good times that much better. Work hard at it; be best friends; respect each other; don't bad mouth your spouse; talk things out; and have fun!

A few thoughts on the financial side of marriage:

- Try to be reasonable about the cost of the wedding. It may seem very romantic to have a grand, elaborate wedding but you may be able to use that money for something more substantial such as money toward a down payment on a house. Far be it from me though, to tromp on the desires of a bride! I'm not that dumb.

- I part ways with many financial planners when I say <u>DO</u> go on a nice honeymoon. Spend **your money on memories not stuff**. You will have the memories and pictures of your honeymoon to reminisce about when you are old and gray and you can see how good you looked when you were young. Just don't go too far in debt for your honeymoon. Save for it prior to the wedding! You can go to an all-inclusive in the Caribbean for a reasonable cost and a cruise is also a nice way to see several different places in a short time and you can get ideas for future trips (Coki Bay in St. Thomas has a beautiful beach and good snorkeling and we love the Palladium resort in Playacar, Mexico).

- After the honeymoon is a good time to start practicing the good budgeting habits laid out earlier. I suggest one of two methods for managing dual paychecks:

    1. Keep your separate checking accounts but change them both to joint accounts and have your respective pay direct deposited into each account. In addition, set up a third checking account from which you pay your bills. After you have equitably divided the regular expenses by your respective ability to pay them, you each will transfer your portion of these expenses into this third

account and this account will ONLY be used to pay expenses. OR:

2. (This how we do it) Keep your separate checking accounts but change them both to joint accounts and have your respective pay direct deposited into each account. After you have equitably divided the regular expenses by your respective ability to pay them, you each pay that portion of the expenses from each account. For example, when we were first married, we paid the house payment out of my wife's account and the rest of the regular expenses out of my account. Our incomes were similar and this method divided these expenses about 50/50. We each paid our respective car insurance, but we tried to keep all expenses allocated this way and it has worked to this day!

3. For large purchases (those above say $500) you both should discuss these purchases and decide how to pay for them. As I said earlier, it would be a bad idea to say "hey, honey, come see my new motorcycle" when you have a water bill, gas bill and rent payment due. Don't make trouble for yourself.

- Start building your emergency savings account. Place this money in a safe account where you can access it if you need it without any delays or fees; this would be a savings account or a money market account.
- Each of you should contribute to whatever kind of retirement plan your employer offers. As a public safety employee, you may be contributing up to 12.25% of your pay to the public pension system unless you have pension pickup by your employer. If you have a spouse in the private sector, he/she probably doesn't have a pension plan but often may have a 401(k) plan or a 403(b) if he/she works in a public school system or a hospital system. If the employer offers to match some portion of your contribution, you should contribute enough of your own money to get this match—**THIS IS FREE MONEY! TAKE ADVANTAGE OF IT!**
- This is a good start. You are establishing good habits early in your marriage and building a foundation for accumulating wealth. These steps will go a long way toward preventing arguments over money, which are the cause of many divorces; **pre-plan now to prevent later trouble**. I will discuss additional investing tactics and strategies a little later. If you have done these steps, congratulate yourself and go out for a nice dinner!

69

You're Going to Have a Baby—Holy Crap!

Having kids reminded me why I didn't want to have kids.
~ Anonymous

Having children made us look differently at all these things
we take for granted, like taking your child to get a vaccine
against measles or polio.
~ Melinda Gates

Let me get a couple of things out of the way: we don't have
children so there will be no child rearing advice from me.
Just an aside: I **hate** the phrase "we are pregnant" coming
from a man—your wife is pregnant and if you get pregnant,
you will become filthy rich and won't need this book! I
helped deliver a baby in the back of our medic truck and all
the father did was sit there and ask us if we knew what we
were doing—**HE** most assuredly was NOT pregnant (and we
knew what we were doing).

Ok, with that off my chest let us agree that having children
fundamentally and forever changes your life. Financially,
you will spend thousands raising your child over the next
eighteen years or so (and who knows how much if they move
back in after college). I am going to comment on two
general areas of your child rearing finances: setting a good
example in your financial habits and saving for college.

In general, I can think of no better way to teach your children good financial habits other than to set a good example by following the concepts laid out in this book and whatever other resources you access (I include a list of suggested resources and reading in the appendix). Some general behaviors you may implement in order to help your children develop good financial habits are:

- Pay them a small amount for doing chores; this way they learn that they earn money through labor or accomplishment.
- Require that they save some portion of all earned money and gifts—get the habit of saving started early.
- Teach them about interest and compound interest when they are old enough to understand.
- When they are older, encourage them to have some kind of paying job so they can develop good work habits unless this interferes with extra-curricular activities or their school work.
- Have them open a savings and checking account and teach them how to use them.
- Teach them about investing if you are comfortable with investing or help them find some good sources on investing. There is no end to good resources to learn financial skills geared to all ages.
- When/if they go to college, provide them with a limited credit card so they have to budget how they spend their limited funds. Now is a good time to learn to live within their means.

- Money is not root of evil; it is a tool that they need to learn how to use effectively. There is nothing inherently wrong with wanting to be wealthy.
- Don't spoil them but don't be too hard either—if they are in a jam, help them out of it but teach them to avoid the behavior/choices that got them into the jam to begin with.
- Well, I fibbed a little bit about child rearing advice by including this piece of advice, but I was fortunate to have two wonderful parents who gave us the proper amounts of love and discipline and I suggest you try to do the same.

Most parents begin to think about paying for college soon after the baby arrives. There are a number of ways to save for college and many resources available to learn about them and you have some time to become knowledgeable about them (check out www.finaid.com). The one I will mention is the Qualified Tuition Plan (QTP) or 529 plan that most all states offer. These are a wonderful savings vehicle for college. The basics of a QTP (as of 2014) are:

- The money you put in may be state income tax deductible to the donor.
- The funds grow tax deferred.
- The money can be used for tuition, fees, books, supplies, equipment, room and board, and expenses for special needs services.
- The money can be used for undergraduate or graduate school.

72

These are just some of the general benefits of a QTP. You can set up a plan with any state's plan and will have to contact the state agency administering the plan for details. There are financial planners and brokers who can set up the plan for you but they will generally charge a fee for doing so. This is something you can do yourself with a little work; it is not rocket science.

My last piece of advice on saving for your children's college, and I repeat myself here, is this: **save and invest for your retirement before saving for college expenses**. There are many ways to pay for college but only you are responsible for your retirement. On this point I really believe that most financial planners would agree with me. This may a good time to see a professional financial planner who charges by the hour to do some long range planning and number crunching.

Be It Ever So Humble: Your Home

The ache for home lives in all of us, the safe place where we
can go as we are and not be questioned.
~ Maya Angelou

I really like the quote above. Home should be a refuge from
the craziness of your job taking care of the public. Owning a
house (I say house because a building is not a home—people
make it a home—only realtors refer to uninhabited structures
as homes) has been described for a long time as "the
American Dream." My wife and I bought our house in 1986
after living in an apartment for two years and it was an
interesting process. Everyone kept telling us that we could
afford more house than we were looking for and that the
neighborhood we ultimately decided to buy in on the far
south side of Columbus, OH was a "bad market." Let me
digress and tell you about our "bad neighborhood."

We have had, with one exception, wonderful neighbors who
look out for each other. We have watched our neighbors'
children grow up and move on in life. We have no bland,
monotonous, cookie cutter houses on our streets. We can
safely walk our streets. We have lots of trees! My wife can
have her garden and clothes line without checking with a
homeowners' association. There have been some minor
vandalism, loud cars, and mouthy teens but those are not
unique to our neighborhood. We live very close to several
stores and we do not have the headache inducing traffic that
is present in the "hot neighborhoods." And our property

74

taxes are much lower than those in the trendy suburbs as are our water and sewer bills.

My points are these:

> Although you may pay more for your house than any other single asset, it is not really your biggest investment—it is not really an investment at all. It is a place to live and raise your family. Now, many people insist that real estate is the best investment "because they aren't making any more of it," but actually they are building more structures everyday—they're not making any more land.

> Buy your house because it is in the neighborhood you want to live in; it is in the school district where you want to send your kids; you just like the house; and you can comfortably afford it. I included a formula earlier in the book in the debt chapter related to house ownership: Monthly mortgage payments (principal, interest, taxes and insurance) should not exceed 28% of gross income or one week's take-home pay.

> For example: your gross income is $65,000 per year so your monthly payments should not exceed $18,200 or $1516 per month. I maintain that you should try to be well under the amount of payment based on this formula. If you are earning $65,000 per year before taxes that is somewhere around $48,000 net take home pay; a $1516 per month mortgage payment would consume 38% of your take home

pay—that leaves you $2484 per month for ALL of your remaining expenses! Please don't start your life "house rich and cash poor."

You may say "but I can borrow against my house for extra money." That may be true or not. If you buy a house and can put down 20% then you have only 20% equity to borrow against plus any appreciation of your house value but, historically, residential real estate has only appreciated about 4% per year—not very much.

Home equity lines of credit can be a useful tool but not when you are starting out. Please don't be too optimistic about using your house as a credit card— much of the financial crisis of 2008 was based on outlandish, unrealistic "values" of residential real estate. Buy your house for the reasons cited above, not as an investment.

Finally, there is the question of what kind and how long of a mortgage you should take on. If you can afford it and you have a good credit score, now (2014-2015) is a wonderful time to buy a house; rates are very low. Your credit score will be critical in determining the interest rate you can lock in for your loan so protect and build that score fanatically.

Mortgages typically are 15 or 30 years in duration. You can get a slightly lower interest rate on a 15 versus a 30 year mortgage but the payments will be higher—but you will pay substantially less interest over the term of the loan. Another option is an adjustable rate mortgage (ARM) which will have an even lower interest rate but it will adjust based on some other, basic interest rate such as the prime rate. Be sure to clearly understand the terms of the ARM and make sure you can afford the payments if they should adjust upward. An ARM may be suitable for you if you are only going to be in the house for a short time and you plan on moving within the term of the loan. An ARM can also be effective if rates are high and you believe they will fall in the future and you can lock in a lower rate later on a conventional mortgage.

One strategy I think can be effective as you start out is to take out a thirty year loan which will have the lower payment and then pay extra principal each month or make an extra payment each year in order to pay down the loan faster and reduce the amount of interest you pay. This way, should you have some sort of temporary financial setback you always go back to paying the regular, lower payment and remain current on your loan payments. As you build your wealth and earn more in your career, you can consider re-financing your loan at a lower rate.

In sum, there are a lot of variables to consider when you consider your first home purchase. Seek out a good realtor, financial planner or both to assist you in this major decision. Don't go it alone if you are confused or uninformed about the many variables involved in this decision.

I Have a Pension: why Do I Need to Save For Retirement?

I'm retired — goodbye tension, hello pension!
~ Unknown Author

Retirement is the ugliest word in the language.
~ Ernest Hemingway

Regardless of how you feel about retirement (by the way, Hemingway must have <u>really</u> hated retirement since he killed himself before retiring), one of the attractions of public safety service is the pension plans. We may be hesitant to admit this since it seems to dilute the purity of public service motivation, but if you say you don't care about your pension, I believe you'll lie about other things too. Let's just say that we in public safety are fortunate to have a pension plan in place. I won't address the controversy surrounding public pension systems except to say that there are people out there who fervently want to dismantle the public pension systems (in Ohio, remember Senate Bill 5?), which is one reason to save and invest beyond your pension system.

In the past, retirees may have been able to depend on the "three legged stool" of retirement funding: 1) company pension plan; 2) Social Security; and 3) personal savings and investments. As I am sure you know many companies have discontinued the traditional **defined benefit** pension plans and often replaced them with **defined contribution** plans such as the 401(k) plan. A short definition of these two terms is necessary.

In a traditional **defined benefit** pension plan that many of our parents and/or grandparents enjoyed, the company employed actuaries who determined how much money the company needed to set aside to fund each employee's pension payments based on complicated formulas based on many variables. When the employee retired, he/she received a monthly pension payment based on such variables as longevity with the company, age, compensation and others. Generally, this was a fixed amount (hence the name **defined benefit**) that did not change over time. These plans were funded from company revenues and were very expensive to fund and so many companies have cancelled or completely amended the plans due to the cost.

These pension plans were a wonderful benefit of employment in a time gone by and they provided basic living income for millions of workers and their demise has created a real retirement planning challenge for today's workers.

Many private sector companies have replaced traditional pension plans with defined contribution plans most often a 401(k) plan. In these plans, the employee decides how much to contribute (hence **defined contribution** plan) to the plan and some companies will match a certain percentage of the employee's contribution but they are not mandated to do so. The primary issues with this change to defined contribution plans is that many people will not contribute or contribute too little and they have to choose their own investments within the plan and they are not educated on how to make the best choices for their future.

I include this short discussion of these kinds of plans because we as public safety employees have the best of both worlds: we still have a defined benefit pension plan that includes cost of living increases! And we have access to a defined contribution plan (Ohio Deferred Compensation Plan also called a section 457 plan; the 457 is the section of federal law that allows and defines the plan).

So let's get back to the question posed in the title of this chapter: you have a pension, so why do you need to save outside the pension plan especially if you are contributing your, full employee portion of your pay? Let's use an example for a firefighter: you got into your career around age 25 and you plan to retire after 25 years at age 50 (we will leave out the DROP for now). The following is taken from the Ohio Police and Fire Pension Fund website where you can input your own numbers/circumstances to obtain an estimate of your final pension payment. I used the following assumptions/inputs:

- Career start at age 25 and you are now 35; birth date is 1/31/1979
- Retire at age 50 on 2/1/2029
- Final salary at age 50: $75,000.
- You have no non-contributing years and no military time

- Assume you are married but your wife did not work outside the home (we know she worked damn hard in the home being married to a fire fighter, police officer or EMT)

The results are a monthly pension payment of $3625 for a **single life annuity (SLA)**, which means that you would receive the $3625 payment as long as you are alive, but when you die, your wife would stop receiving the payment. You are hoping (gambling) that you stay alive as long as your wife is alive. **This is a critical and irrevocable decision about your pension.** Statistically, given that women outlive men, you are taking a chance with your wife's standard of living in her retirement years. You must critically consider whether you may outlive her or that she has a separate, sufficient income stream to forego your pension income. I can't stress enough how important this decision is!

If you decide on the **joint and survivor** (JSA) option, you would receive $3213 per month—a lesser amount but your wife would continue to receive this amount for the rest of her life if you die before her. My dad was a teacher and he chose this option when he retired and my mom could not have made it on just her pension so it is a critical decision!

Ok, let's say you choose the JSA option. You will receive a yearly income of $38,556 adjusted for the cost of living for the rest of your life—pretty sweet! BUT you were making $75,000 the year before you retired—how will you make up the difference of $36,444? You ask: don't I get Social

81

Security? Ha! The answer is yes if you had a second job where you paid into the SS system. I will cover Social Security later in the book in more detail but for now let's assume that you will receive a token amount from SS say $500 per month (which you cannot collect until you are at least 62—12 years from now). Now you are up to a yearly income of $42,444 per year (at age 62) and that may be enough to survive on but it certainly won't provide the standard of living you enjoyed when you worked full time.

The key question you need to ask is: **"How much money do I need to maintain the same standard of living I enjoyed when I was working?"** There is no easy answer to this question but there are lots of theories that try to do so. One rule of thumb is that you would want to have an income that will be at least 80% of your pre-retirement income ($75,000 x .8 = $60,000) so for simplicity, let's use that figure as the amount of yearly income you would need in retirement. We have determined that your pension and social security will provide $42,444 per year so where will the remaining $17,556 come from? Now you could and probably will try to find a job after your retirement but again for the sake of illustration let's say you don't want to work anymore so you will need to generate that $17,556 from somewhere and here is where we answer the question posed in the chapter title.

The answer is simple actually: **you will need to save and invest in addition to your pension and social security**. I promised no complicated math so I won't do any here but you will need some amount of savings and investments to generate that extra income. One simple calculation shows you how much you would have to have accumulated to provide the needed amount given a specific interest rate. Example: you need $17,556 and you think you can generate a 3% return on your accumulated savings and investments. To find out how much you would have to accumulate to generate that amount of interest income **without using any of the principal** we simply divide $17,556 by .03 and we come up with $585,200 needed to generate the needed amount.

If you want to also withdraw some of the principal each year you need to do some more complicated planning and calculating and there are financial planning calculators on the internet where you can do this or you can get help from a financial advisor.

In the most basic terms you will derive retirement spending from two kinds of sources: 1) guaranteed income from a regular payment from your pension, Social Security or some similar source or 2) withdrawals from you savings and investments. In the best of worlds, you will have both kinds and that is what you will have if you save beyond your pension. **The critical key to a secure, financial retirement is to create a steady, secure stream of income to replace the income from your working life.**

As you can see from this basic example, the point is this: you will need to save outside your pension plan and whatever social security you will receive (and, to repeat, you can't tap social security until you are at least 62) in order to provide enough income to maintain your standard of living after you retire. So, how, where and how much should you be saving and investing? Next chapter please.

Saving Beyond Your Pension

"Compound interest is the eighth wonder of the world. He who understands it, earns it ... he who doesn't ... pays it."
~ Albert Einstein

I'm not sure how good of an investor Professor Einstein was but let's agree that he did understand math pretty well and had a quantum impact on the twentieth century.

I will repeat some of what I mentioned in the previous investing section here, but it is key, so it bears some extra attention. Your investments outside your pension plan will determine to a large extent the comfort and security of your retirement. Let me repeat and emphasize that point again: **your choices of investments will determine the comfort and security of your retirement**. So what does that mean? In a nutshell: don't screw it up! But don't worry too much—good solid, **long term** investing is not rocket science and you can do it. I emphasize long term investing which means, at a minimum, five years or more and really it means until you decide to retire so based on your age, it may mean twenty-five years or more!

As I emphasized in the introduction to this book, I don't want to clutter it with complicated formulas or theories but I must include some concepts that I and many other investors have found to be true regardless of what you hear the media freaking out about (sorry about that technical jargon of "freaking out"). The following are some beliefs, truisms,

www.vsfinsvs.com

and lessons I have learned and believe in based on my twenty-eight years of investing and studying investing.

- A famous economist, John Maynard Keynes, once said, "In the long run we all are dead." True enough. But when I say "long term" I mean from the time you start investing to the time you need to withdraw that money to spend. You simply must have a long term investing horizon so that short term "noise" (like CNBC) doesn't deter you or frighten you from concentrating on you ultimate goal: enough wealth to provide the kind of retirement you want!
- Over the long term, common stocks will provide the best growth potential for your invested money. When you own stocks, you own part of a business or many businesses if you own a mutual fund or an exchange traded fund (ETF). This is not my opinion. Volumes of research confirm this conviction (see the appendix for a list of books for further study and evidence). I include a historical chart of the Standard and Poors 500 chart below to illustrate the inevitable, upward direction of this index of common stocks.

The S&P 500 consists of the stocks of the 500 largest companies in the United States and has changed over time but it is a commonly accepted proxy for the US stock market. Yes, there have been ups and downs (called volatility) but the trend has always been up in the long run. I have experienced three of the largest stock market "crashes" in history, 1987, 2000 and

2008 and yet here late in 2014 the stock market is at historical highs and I am glad I didn't follow the "smart money" managed by professionals and sell when the markets were down.

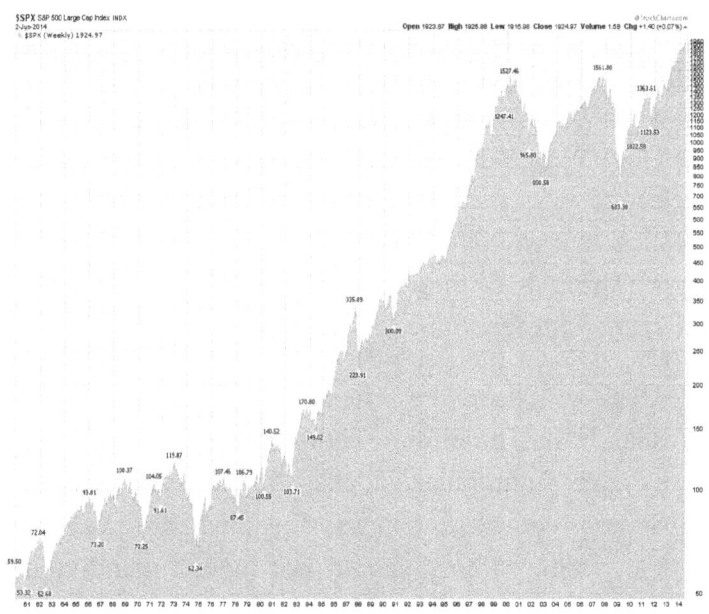

One quote by Dave Ramsey that I love concerns the volatility in the stock market and how the media loves to fixate on and sensationalize volatility and how they often compare the stock market to a roller coaster ride: "You only get hurt if you jump off the roller coaster." Absolutely true! **You cannot time the market**.

There are many academic studies and anecdotal evidence showing that too many investors sell when the market is down and buy when it is very high by trying to time the market. You must regularly invest a set amount of money

87

and leave your money in the market to grow. Don't check the stock market every day—daily changes are simply emotional reactions by millions of people to events of the day.

I love history and here is a very brief history lesson: since 1900, the United States has experienced a war in the Philippines, WWI, the Great Depression, WWII, the Korean War, the Cold War, Vietnam, the First Gulf War, September 11, the Second Iraq War, several stock market bubbles, the great real estate bubble, and most recently the Great Recession. Through all these horrific and frightening events the stock market has continued its upward trend.

- Unless you have the education, time, and drive to research and monitor individual companies, do not invest in individual stocks. Now, this kind of investing can be fun, interesting and profitable, but most people simply should not invest in individual stocks. Should you decide that you want to try your hand at individual stock investing, I suggest you join Better Investing (www.betterinvesting.org) and/or the American Association of Individual Investors (www.aaii.com) both of which are non-profit, educational organizations dedicated to education for individual investors.

- So what should you invest in? For your core, basic investment, you should invest in index mutual funds or index exchange traded funds that track the S&P 500. The common traits of these funds are that they hold shares of the 500 largest companies in the

United States, they have very low management fees (low fees are critical to your long term results—the lower, the better) and you can purchase them for very low commissions or from some brokerages, with no commissions at all!

- What about income and/or bonds? I really believe, and I differ from "conventional wisdom" here, that if you are twenty or more years from retirement, you don't need to own any bonds unless your taxable income is so high that you may need some tax free income from tax free bonds but most young public sector members don't have that kind of income.

  o "Conventional wisdom" says that you should subtract your age from 100 and the remainder number is the percentage of stocks you should have in your portfolio. For example: you are twenty-five so 100-25=75 so you should have a portfolio of 75% stocks and 25% bonds. The reasoning is that this mix will smooth out volatility in the shorter term, **but remember that we are saving for the long term future and we don't care about the short term**. You will give up a lot of potential profit if you invest that much in bonds since stocks have returned much more over time than bonds (see John Stewart' s Law number 4, the Law of Concentration). This is my belief and you can find a lot of literature arguing against it but again, it's my book. I welcome your questions and challenges on this point.

o Traditionally, bonds are included in a portfolio to produce income—well, you will be receiving a pension that provides you with income that adjusts upward with inflation so you will not need bonds to provide you with this income.

- Find the lowest cost investments, which just happen to be index funds and index ETFs. Keeping your costs as low as possible will have significant positive results over time. This is a fact and there is **overwhelming** evidence supporting it. Case closed.

Sorry—Some Basic Math for Investment Planning

If you read any investing literature or listen to any business television, you will hear the term "investment return" often accompanied by some historical averages. There are different kinds of investment returns, some of which are more accurate than others but the key concept is that return is the growth of your invested funds over some given time interval. One of the most common, yearly growth rate discussed is the return of common stocks over time and the most common value offered is 10% give or take a half percent and this is a historically, accurate, **average** return.

Caveats: This is the **average, historical** return for large, common stocks and there is no guarantee that future returns will be in the 10% neighborhood, which has been a pretty good neighborhood. This 10% return has not been a steady 10% each year but it has varied, often by significant amounts, over time so again you have to have a long term perspective and have the discipline not to sell when Mr. Market declines but to have the courage to buy when he puts his goods on sale.

So what are my point(s)? When planning for you future you must decide on and input an expected return for your investments so you can decide what amount of money you need to invest on a regular basis in order to achieve **your** objectives.

I believe you need to decide on a fairly conservative return for one very important reason: if you project that you can achieve a 12% yearly, compounded return (as one famous radio and book personality does, although he won't tell you the specific investments he purchased in order to attain that 12%) you don't need to save as much to invest since compound interest will let you earn more with a lesser savings rate.

Example: say you want to accumulate $500,000 in 25 years and you are able to invest the needed amount on January 1 of each year.

At a 12% compounded return, you need to invest $3348.20 each year.

At an 8% compounded return, you need to invest $6332.77 each year—quite a difference! (all calculations done with an HP 10BII financial calculator)

My point is that if you are too optimistic in your expected return, what happens if you don't earn that return or worse, you try to time the market, that is you try to buy when it is low and sell when it is high--which NO ONE has been able to do consistently--you will not achieve your goal. A yearly investment of $3348.20 at 10% would produce just $362,214—a shortfall of $137,786 from just a 2% lower return!

Now let's say you are cautious and invest the $6332.77 and you achieve a 10% return rather than the 8% you projected, then you would accumulate $685,920! Wow, better to be surprised on the upside than the downside! You or you and a good financial adviser must decide what you expect to earn from your mix of investments and stick to your plan. **Disciplined saving and consistent investing will serve you better in the long run than most any other strategy**.

Please do your planning and be realistic. Your definition of success should be that you accumulate the wealth that you require to live your life the way you want, not to beat some arbitrary percentage return.

Second Jobs

Be an Employee or Work For Yourself?

This section may apply more to firefighters than to other public safety members since many firefighters have several days off, however many public safety professionals may start a business after they retire. Setting up your own business can be personally rewarding as well as financially advantageous. You will be your own boss and no officer can tell you what to do! You can work at something that you find rewarding or fun. If you are not the entrepreneurial type, you may simply want to get a second job for extra income. Let's start with just getting a second job and list some advantages:

- Obviously, extra income.
- Contribution to social security (more discussion on SS later).
- Possible availability of a retirement plan, e.g. a 401(k) plan.
- Possible chance to buy stock in the company at a discount, say if you work for a company like Lowes.
- Just doing work different from the stressful work you do in public safety.

Starting your own business WILL be a lot of work and you MUST be self-motivated. I suggest doing some research on self employment and on the specific business you want to start. Self-employment can be very rewarding personally

93

and financially. Here is what I have learned from starting my own business and from extensive reading about successful business people. There are many, really good books available to help you start a business, both general information and books specific to your chosen business type.

- Don't reinvent the wheel! Read, research and talk to business owners. It's been done before so learn from those who have gone before you.

- Do some soul searching about what you want to do; if you don't enjoy it, you probably won't be successful at it.

- You must be a "numbers" person and be willing to set up a good business process and organization (watch "Shark Tank" or "The Profit" on CNBC and notice what these very successful business people focus on). I discovered that famous business owners like John D. Rockefeller and Andrew Carnegie obsessed about costs and keeping their costs to the minimum necessary. I don't advocate treating your employees as badly as Carnegie did at times, but you need to know how much you are spending and how much you are bringing in. I can't stress this enough: if you don't like doing the "numbers/accounting" work, find a good bookkeeper and/or tax preparer to do it for you! This will be money well spent come tax time.

- Be sure to set up your business so you limit your personal liability, which means incorporation in some form—don't be a sole proprietor. It is not complicated or expensive to do this.

- Be sure you have adequate start-up capital and operating capital for your first couple of years since it may take some time to become profitable.

- There are many tax advantages for you in owning a business. I won't go into detail because much of this would depend on the kind of business you choose and you should seek out a good accountant and/or contact a member of the Tax Coach™ business tax planning system for thorough tax planning advice that could save you a lot of money in tax avoidance (avoiding taxes is perfectly legal whereas tax evasion can get you a visit from the IRS).

- You will contribute to Social Security which will add retirement income.

I'm not going to say much more than this since I am not an expert (but I'm learning more each day) on starting a business but I think the previous points are a good starting point. A business may be the perfect complement to your job in public safety.

Closing In On Retirement

Yes, retirement—wow it really did happen way too fast or not fast enough depending on your view. So let's say you are in your forties and you are thinking about retirement. I'll start with a short list of things to be thinking about at this point. Remember, you need to think about these things well before your year of retirement.

- When/what age do you want to retire?
- How is your health? How long can you do the job?
- Do you want to enter the DROP if you are eligible?
- What do you plan on doing after retirement?
- How are your finances? Are you on target to accumulate the needed funds for your retirement?
- Have you done the needed financial planning to determine how much you will need in retirement?
- If you are short of where you need to be in your life/career, what are you going to do to make up the difference?
- You may consider purchasing Long Term Care Insurance. This kind of insurance pays for extended stays in care facilities and sometimes for in home care. The premiums are expensive and get more expensive as you get older. There are a lot of variables that go into deciding whether to purchase this kind of insurance and I strongly suggest you talk to a financial planner who is not a seller of insurance

to get an objective discussion of the merits and weaknesses of buying this insurance.

I will repeat a section from my investing chapter here because it still applies: in the book, <u>The Millionaire Next Door</u>, the authors provide a formula for determining what your net worth ought to be: **multiply your age times your realized pretax annual household income from all sources except inheritances. Divide by ten. This, less an inherited wealth, is what your net worth should be.** If you are close or over this number, great—go out for dinner! If not, time to get to work. I will return to "fix-it" strategies later. Let's look at each of the above items:

<u>When/what age do you want to retire?</u>

A lot of variables go into this decision. One that may affect public safety workers may be simply what is your job at this time? Are you in an office job or are you still "on the street"? I think this leads directly to a crucial question: **how is your health?** Can you continue to do what can be a very physical job at times or are you in an office where you don't have to do physical work anymore? **Regardless, one of, if not the most important action you can take in your life is to take care of your health!** This ain't complicated: stop smoking or using any kind of tobacco if you do it now—it is just down right, no question, stupid to use tobacco of **any** kind; exercise; eat a good, balanced diet low in carbohydrates; use alcohol in moderation and wear your seat belt for crying out loud.

Do you want to enter the DROP plan if you are eligible? It is hard to argue against the financial advantage to entering the DROP plan so your decision will depend on other, non-financial factors such as how much longer do you want to work and again is your health good so you will be able to enjoy that extra money when you do hang it up.

What do you plan to do after you retire? A lot of research has been done on how to create a successful retirement and one of the most critical elements researchers have identified is what you choose to do in retirement. Most likely, you will still be relatively young and so playing golf or fishing every day really isn't a realistic goal. Again, there are a lot of good books about how to create YOUR version of a great retirement and some of the common themes are: start a small business; start a second career in something you love; volunteer; and, travel, of course. The key is to have a plan of what you want to do to create a fulfilling retirement.

Now, the "money" questions: Have you done the needed financial planning to determine how much you will need in retirement? If you are short of where you need to be in your life/career, what are you going to do to make up the difference?

Save more: this is self evident. You will simply have to save more if you are short. You will have do some serious examination of your spending and decide where you can cut back and increase your saving. Again, there are some very good books available on reducing debt and increasing savings.

98

<u>More stock investing</u>: based on financial history, you should be able to achieve greater growth of your wealth by investing more of your money in common stocks. The obvious caveat is that in the short term there is more risk of paper losses but if you have over five years until retirement, you should be able to achieve greater appreciation of your investments in common stocks versus other investments.

<u>Plan on working during retirement</u>: if you don't feel comfortable investing in common stocks or you can't find extra money to save, you may need to work after your public safety career is over. If this is your situation, you may need to obtain some extra training and/or education and learn new skills (good computer skills almost will be a must, and I don't mean gaming).

Hope like hell you get a huge inheritance or you win the lottery. Good luck with that; but not a realistic strategy.

www.vsfinsvs.com

Now, How Do You Spend What You Have Saved?

I tell my clients that the last check they write should be to the undertaker...and that it should bounce.
~ Stephen Pollan, Author of <u>Die Broke</u>.

This may seem like a dumb question—you just spend what you have, right? Actually, safely and effectively spending your retirement resources may be more complicated than accumulating them. Again, there is a lot of innovative, academic research being done that is examining the most effective ways to spend your retirement resources so that you do not run out of money before you die. Other research demonstrates that running out of money before dying is the greatest fear of retirees.

For many years the default solution recommended for spending a retirement portfolio was to spend 4% each year and increase that percentage by the amount of inflation each year. You will often see this recommendation in popular finance magazines and in many retirement books.

Subsequent research is challenging this standard and is demonstrating that the calculation may be more complicated. I won't go into all the studies and theories but I can say this: this is a serious issue that you will find it worthwhile to discuss with a professional, financial planner. It will be the most delicate balancing act in your retirement deciding how

100

much to spend to enjoy retirement but not spending too much too soon and running out of money before you die.

In support of my above recommendation, I include a short list of issues and questions that you much consider and make some assumptions about.

- Are your assets in a taxable, tax-deferred or tax free account(s)?
- If so, how much is in each kind of account?
- What are the percentages of your retirement resources in stocks, bonds, cash or other assets respectively?
- What **should be** the percentages of your retirement resources in stocks, bonds, cash or other assets respectively?
- How much guaranteed income (pension, annuity, Social Security) will you receive and at what age(s)?
- What do you estimate your income tax rate will be when you retire?
- What do you estimate inflation will be in the future?
- Will you be receiving an inheritance?
- Finally, do you feel competent and confident in answering these questions? If not, get help—a small investment now in good planning will reap a lifetime of benefits.

Social Security and Public Sector Employment

I started my working career in the printing industry and worked for thirteen years in that business and in that time I earned my 40 credits to fully vest me in the Social Security system so I should get a nice pension payout and my Social Security to boot—sweet right? Wrong. First, a little basic history and context.

Social Security was established during the 1930s as part of many financial reform programs proposed and passed by the Roosevelt administration in response to the Great Depression. Social Security's goal was to provide a minimal stipend that would complement a retiree's savings and other resources in order to provide a basic, secure retirement; the ultimate goal was simply to prevent retirees from living in abject poverty—a worthy goal.

Of course, in the 1930s most people were not expected to live much beyond the established retirement age of 65 (average life expectancy for all races and sexes in 1940 was 62.9), and it was not intended to provide a full living wage in retirement. In 2014, however, life expectancy is much longer and Social Security is a critical component of retirement planning.

If a retiree worked in the private sector, his/her SS computations are straight-forward, even if the decision when to actually begin receiving SS payments is not always straight-forward. For those of us in the public sector who earn wages/salaries that are not subject to SS withholding, the rules are different. We are subject to two provisions called the Windfall Elimination Provision (WEP) and the Government Pension Offset (GPO) that reduce the SS payment we can receive. The SS Administration provides two, brief explanatory documents at their website if you want to know more (www.ssa.gov), however here is a brief description/explanation.

WEP: SS multiplies your earnings by percentages for three different levels of earnings and combines the results to determine your monthly payment. If you are covered by a pension earned from a job where your earnings were not subject to SS withholding, these percentages are reduced, which then reduces your payment.

There are some exceptions, primarily if you earned "substantial "earnings in a job where you paid SS on those wages; for example, in 2014 "substantial" earnings are any above $21,750. The key issue is that unless you had substantial earnings during your working life, you will receive a reduced SS benefit so you must plan for this. I suggest you use the calculator and charts on the SS website (www.socialsecurity.gov/retire2/wep-chart.htm) or use a software product available on the internet (I use Maximize My Social Security at www.maximizemysocialsecurity.com, which costs $40 to use). There are other websites and products to determine your SS payment under the WEP.

There is a movement in Congress to eliminate the WEP and it may have a chance in the new Congress and we will just have to wait.

Some may see this as getting "screwed" but I do not. You did not pay into the SS system so why should you receive a full benefit from it? Your public sector pension payment will be much more generous than your SS payment would have been. Just my opinion, and again, it is my book.

GPO (Government Pension Offset) This is a law that affects spouses and widows or widowers. Briefly, this provision mandates that "if you receive a pension from a federal, state, or local government ...your Social Security spouse's or widow's or widower's benefits may be reduced."

The rules state that this reduction will be two-thirds of your government pension. The example provided by the SS web site is: if you receive a monthly $600 public pension payment and your wife/husband would normally be eligible for a $500 SS monthly payment, that $500 would be reduced by 2/3 of your public pension payment or $400 and you would receive $100 from SS.

If your spouse worked in a job where he/she paid into SS, he/she will still receive his/her full SS payment based on his/her earnings. The GPO affects only dependent benefits.

Regardless of the above provisions, if you and/or your spouse are going to receive Social Security in retirement, you need to learn about the different strategies available to maximize your ultimate benefits. As I mention in the

104

appendix, I use a software program call "Maximize My Social Security" which is very thorough and comprehensive in providing you with the strategy for maximizing your benefits. If you or someone you know is close to claiming Social Security I strongly urge you to visit this site or you can contact me and I can perform the same service for you at a reasonable fee.

Be Warned: if you do not choose wisely you can leave a lot of money on the table so don't be like the bad guy in the third "Raiders of The Lost Ark" movie because as you remember, he chose poorly and his face melted off.

You're Close to Retirement

Don't Be Putting Out Fires

No funny quotes here. Even if you are not a firefighter, you still understand the analogy; **you simply must prepare for retirement well before your retirement date!** <u>**You must!**</u> Many people will spend more time planning a vacation than planning their retirement. There are a lot of books, computer programs, web sites and other sources of retirement planning information out there for you to access. Just to get you thinking about much of what we have covered, here are some basic steps you need to take.

If you have not accumulated substantial assets, make sure you have enough life insurance to provide for your family if something would happen to you.

<u>Start saving and investing as early as you can.</u> In your twenties and thirties, you simply need to be saving and investing. You can do some basic calculations to estimate how much you will receive from your pension and consequently how much you need to accumulate to complement this amount. These two primary income stream sources will provide the bulk of your retirement income.

<u>Save and invest for your retirement before funding college for your children.</u> Most, if not all financial advisers, recommend this strategy for one basic reason. There are many ways to provide and afford a college education but there are very few options if you haven't planned, saved and

invested enough to provide you with sufficient income for your retirement.

<u>Live within your means!</u> I can't stress this enough. Try to avoid "bad" debt and buy smart—pay cash if you can. Buy a used car; live in a smaller house; and simply learn how to keep you expenses less than your income. Being debt free (except for your mortgage) is a wonderful feeling.

<u>Try to envision your retirement.</u> Will you continue working in another career or start your own business? Do you want to travel? Try to estimate how much income you will require to live the retirement you want. It's not really retirement, but a transition to a new phase of your life. Much research shows that you will spend much more in the early years (up to about age 70) than later on.

Conclusions

I have enjoyed writing this and I hope it has been of some help for you. All the answers are not in here because I don't and I'm sure no one has all the answers—just watch any financial show and watch the friction between the "experts." I love the financial world and will until I die. I have spent a lot of time in the past twenty eight years reading journals, magazines, books, and web sites and attending many conferences on investing, financial planning and tax planning/preparation and have soaked up a lot of information and knowledge.

I wrote this book to help you, the public safety professional, get your financial life in a little better shape. You engage in training on a regular basis to hone your skills and learn new skills and I encourage you to get involved in your financial life. It is a cliché, but true: **no one cares as much about your money as you do**.

Most people, for a variety of reasons, neglect their financial affairs or make ineffective choices like keeping all their money in a savings account rather than investing some time and money in putting together a plan. If you are ready to plan for your financial future, I would really like to talk with you. Even if you choose not to work with me, I can introduce you to other people with whom you may want to work. **The MOST important goal of this book is to get you to take action!** You have been the "helper" during your

108

career so don't be afraid to ask for some help so you can do your best to avoid having pure chance and/or luck determine your financial future.

BE SAFE OUT THERE!

Acknowledgements

First of all I want to thank Ed Lyon, co-owner of the Tax Coach tax planning system for challenging me to write this book. He gave me a deadline of January 1, 2015 which was a little too soon, but I could never face him again if I had not finished it.

I also must thank John Stewart who graciously agreed to read the book and offer suggestions for improvement and for allowing me to include his laws of investing. Thank you John!

Finally, I want to thank my wife Mary for trusting me to invest our meager assets many years ago and trusting that time, frugality and compound interest would eventually provide the retirement and life she deserves. We are getting close to our retirement, but looking forward to enjoying what we have worked hard to achieve. I love you very much!

www.vsfinsvs.com

FURTHER RESOURCES FOR INFORMATION AND EDUCATION

The following list is not exhaustive of the books I have read and consulted in my financial career, nor is it intended just to impress you (well, maybe a little bit?). Anyone who is passionate about a subject will have a similar and often more extensive reading list. These are the sources that I have found to stand the test of time, easy to read and to understand. Some are true "classics" in the financial literature and I will note these.

Basic Financial Planning
BOOKS

The Wealthy Barber by David Chilton

The Millionaire Next Door by Thomas J Stanley, Ph.D. and William D. Danko, Ph.D. (Classic)

Die Broke by Steven M. Pollan and Mark Levine

The Truth About Money by Ric Edelman (Classic)

The Joy of Financial Security by Donna Skeels Cygan

Spend 'til The End by Laurence J. Kotlifoff and Scott Burns

Why Smart People Do Stupid Things With Money by Bert Whitehead

The Total Money Makeover by Dave Ramsey

The Behavior Gap by Carl Richards

Don't Sweat the Small Stuff…and it's all small stuff by Richard Carlson, Ph.D. this is just a good book for keeping life in perspective.

Any book by Mike Piper

The Financial Wisdom of Ebenezer Scrooge by Ted Klontz, Rick Kahler, and Brad Klontz. A fun, quick, wise look at your relationship with money.

Your Money and Your Brain by Jason Zweig. A good explanation of the science of behavioral finance.

Cold Hard Truth on Men, Women and Money by Kevin O'Leary ("Mr. Wonderful" on the TV show Shark Tank).

For a financial planner who charges by the hour look at the Garrett Network at www.garrettplanningnetwork.com. Membership requirements to be in this organization are stringent and you can be sure of the quality of the planners in this network.

MAGAZINES

"Money Magazine"

"Kiplinger Magazine"

Debt Reduction

Pay It Down by Jean Chatsky (any book by Jean Chatsky is worthwhile)

Total Money Makeover by Dave Ramsey

www.vsfinsvs.com

Investing

Understanding Wall Street by Jeffrey Little and Lucien Rhodes (Classic)

The Intelligent Investor by Benjamin Graham (Classic) Professor Graham was Warren Buffet's teacher. I suggest you get the revised edition by Jason Zweig

A Random Walk Down Wall Street by Burton G. Malkiel (Classic)

Stocks For The Long Run by Professor Jeremy Siegel (Classic)

The Intelligent Asset Allocator by William Bernstein

Are You a Stock or Bond? by Moshe A. Milevsky, Ph. D. Professor Milevsky offers a little different view on the kinds of investing that is appropriate for your level of comfort with stock market investing.

The ETF Book by Richard A. Ferri, CFA Rick Ferri is a die hard believer in passive, index investing and this book will teach you more than you ever wanted to know about ETFs.

All About Asset Allocation by Richard A. Ferri.

ASSOCIATIONS

Better Investing at www.betterinvesting.com

The American Association of Individual Investors at www.aaii.com

Business Start Up Help

The E-Myth Revisited by Michael E. Gerber

Second Act Careers by Nancy Collamer, MS

Retirement

The New Retire-mentality by Mitch Anthony

Die Broke by Steven M. Pollan and Mark Levine

The Truth About Retirement Plans and IRAs by Ric Edelman

The State and Local Government Workers' Retirement Savings Guide by Bruce Stuart

Get What's Yours by Laurence Kotlikoff, Phillip Moeller and Paul Solman. Brand new book that covers Social Security in depth. Has gotten great reviews.

Software
Quicken: I love Quicken for keeping detailed and comprehensive financial records for everything. I currently am using the 2013 version and have seen very bad reviews of Quicken 2014 and 2015 on Amazon so you might want to look at some competing products.

Moneydance: learned about this on Amazon. Haven't used it so I'm going by the reviews on Amazon.

Mint.com I have seen very good reviews of this web site for detailed money management.

ES Planner: (www.esplanner.com) I use this program which is based on the theories presented in Spend 'til The End by Laurence J. Kotlikoff and Scott Burns. You can buy the software or use the online version for free.

Maximize My Social Security: (www.maximizemysocialsecurity.com) also based on Prof. Kotlikoff's work, the site costs $40 and will require you to fill in the data needed to provide you with detailed options for claiming your Social Security benefits. I believe it is well worth the fee. I currently subscribe to the professional version and can perform the analysis for you.

www.ingramcontent.com/pod-product-compliance
Lightning Source LLC
Chambersburg PA
CBHW070817180526
45168CB00002B/651